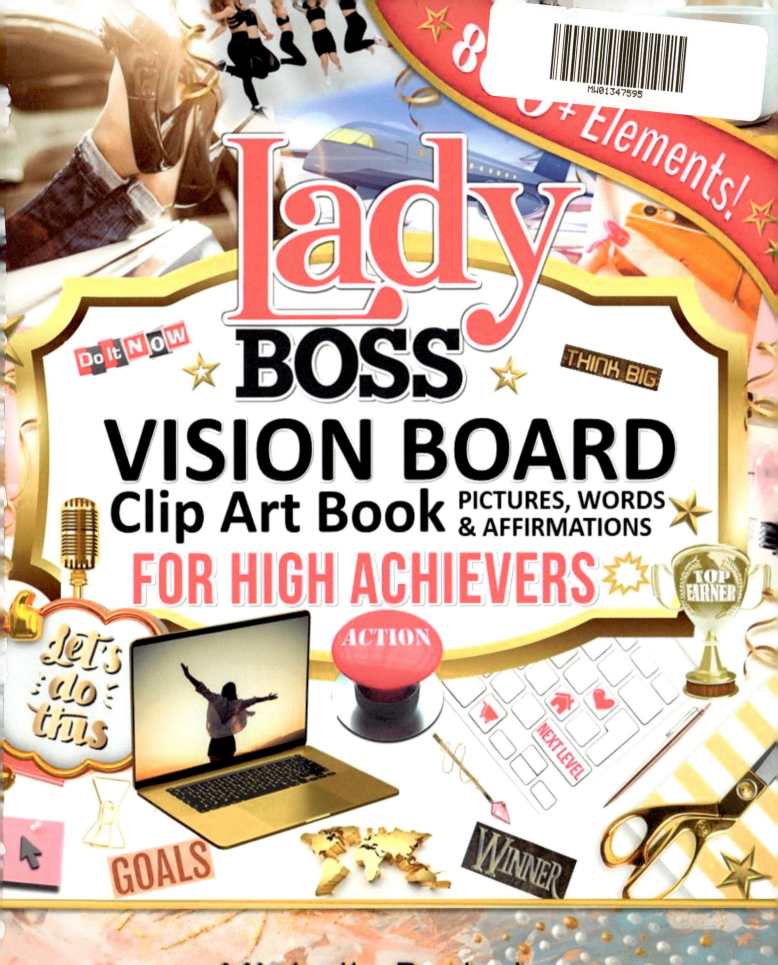

A Note from the Creator

I'm so excited you picked up this book! My *Lady Boss Vision Board Clip Art Book* was so inspiring to create. I hope you love it as much as I do!

Please take a moment to support independent creators like me by reviewing this book on Amazon – I truly appreciate it! ★★★★★

Thank you for purchasing my books!

Michelle Brubaker

✉ hi@michellebrubaker.com

About

Michelle is the creator of the Lady Boss Vision Board Clip Art Book Series. In addition, she is the founder of a best-selling activity book brand selling over 90,000 copies worldwide.

She resides in the beautiful Pacific Northwest USA, enjoys publishing books and inspiring entrepreneurs to build their own successful businesses.

Getting Started
Creating Your Vision Board

1 **Clarify your vision.** Identify your goals, dreams and aspirations. You may want to break it down by categories such as business, career, relationships, family, health, fitness, fun, hobbies, mindfulness, spiritual, home, finances and more!

2 **Decide on a format.** Many visionaries prefer using actual poster boards, but standard paper sizes or even a dashboard in your daily planner can work well too. I've used them all!

3 **Gather and assemble.** Select pictures, words and affirmations that represent your goals and inspire you to success. Cut and paste them onto your board.

Extra tips:
- Use the back pages as extra backgrounds and borders for your goal pictures and words.
- When your vision board is complete, take a picture, then print and post it in even more places to remind you of your goals. You may even enjoy using your vision board picture as a background image on your computer. For more inspiration, you can use the picture as a decorative and motivational wallpaper on your phone or tablet, so you can take it with you on the go.

700+ Words, Quotes & Affirmations

Lady Boss Vision Board Clip Art Book, Volume 2

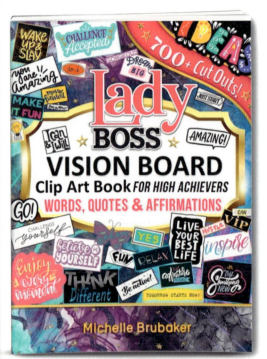

This captivating book features a bright full-color interior adorned with motivational **words, quotes, and affirmations**.

Designed specifically for ambitious women who are driven by their goals!

With a focus on empowering you to become the master of your own destiny, this book includes **over 700+ phrases to cut out** and embrace your inner lady boss.

. . . .

Learn about new releases and download free printable vision board pages!

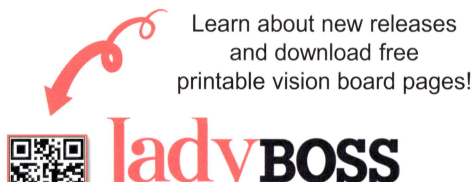

www.LadyBossBooks.com

©2023 Michelle Brubaker
All rights reserved.

No part of this book may be reproduced without permission from the publisher.

Disclaimer: there are no guarantees of your results by using this book. The publisher is not responsible for your success, you are.

For questions or to send a message contact hi@michellebrubaker.com.

BELIEVE IN YOURSELF

The sky is the LIMIT

Fabulous

Don't STOP ME

ENJOY EVERY MOMENT

LIVIN' THE DREAM

I ATTRACT ALL GOOD THINGS

ACTION

Lady BOSS

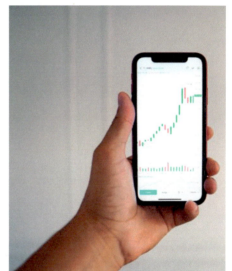

Enjoy Health

Organic

Eat Wise DROP A *Size*

Detox

VEGAN

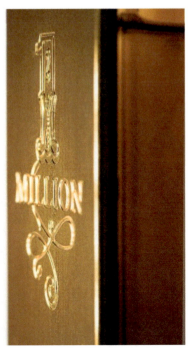

INVEST IN *yourself*

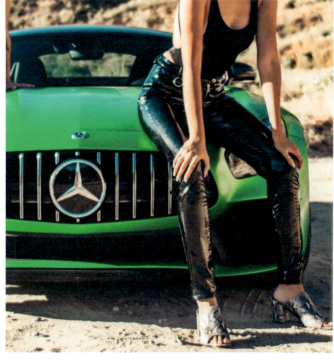

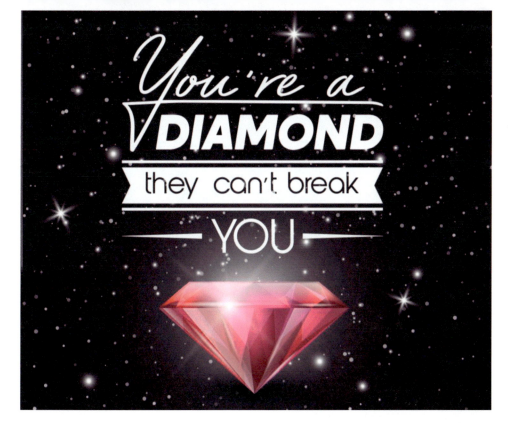

	2815
	Date _____
Pay to the Order of _____	$ [_____]
_____ Dollars	
Memo _____ _____	

⑆85871713⑆ ⑈186358875771⑈ 11638

	2815
	Date _____
Pay to the Order of _____	$ [_____]
_____ Dollars	
Memo _____ _____	

⑆85871713⑆ ⑈186358875771⑈ 11638

	2815
	Date _____
Pay to the Order of _____	$ [_____]
_____ Dollars	
Memo _____ _____	

⑆85871713⑆ ⑈186358875771⑈ 11638

AAAABBBC
CCDDDEEE
EFFFGGGH
HHHIIIIJJJ
KKKLLLM
MMMNNN
OOOOPPP
PQQRRRR

RSSSTTTT
UUUUVW
WWXXYYYY
ZZ11223334
45556677788
9900!!???,.*
""@#$%&+
=(){}<>/~:

2024 Plan
2025 2026
2027 2028
30 Days 90 Days
5 Year Plan
10 Year Plan
20 Year Plan
NEXT NOW

ACTION
BIG MOVE

Travel the world

She's Going **Places!**

Queen
HUSTLE

Growth

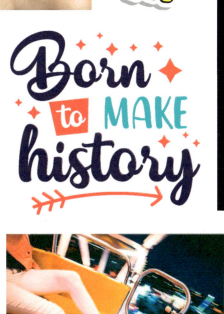

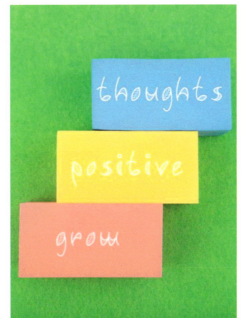

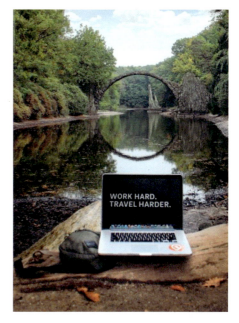
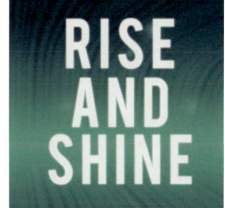

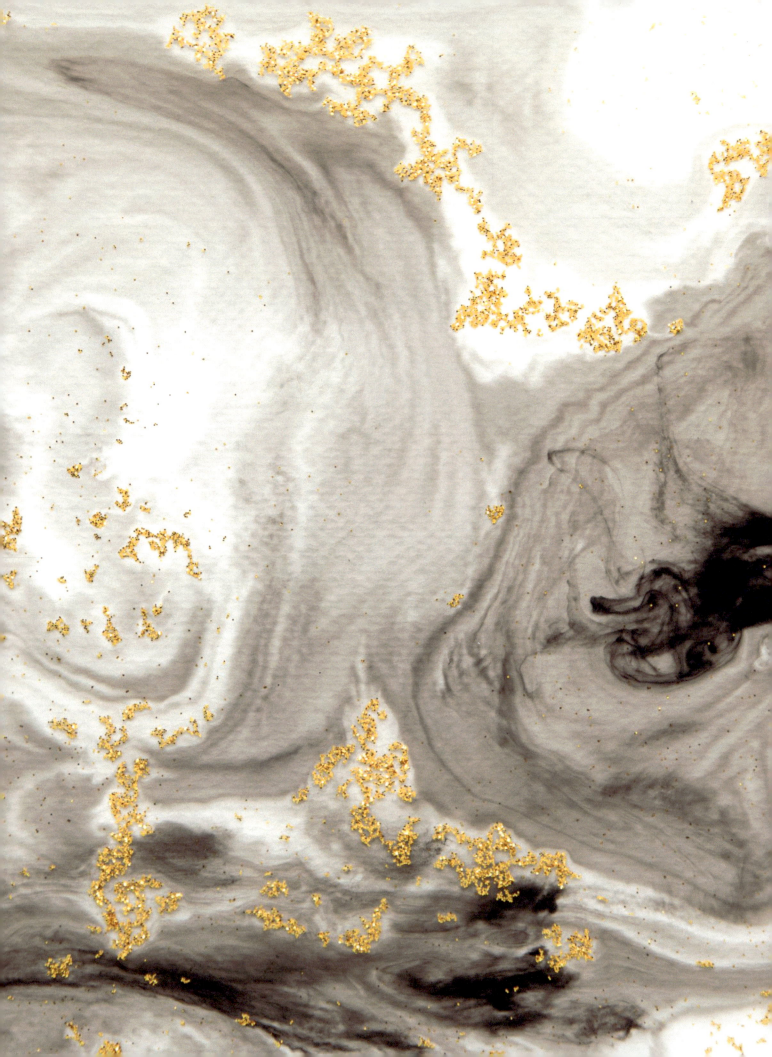

Imagination

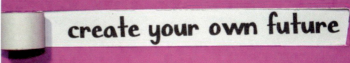

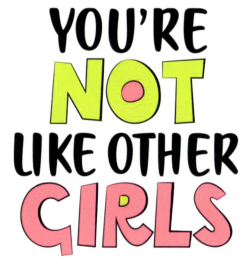

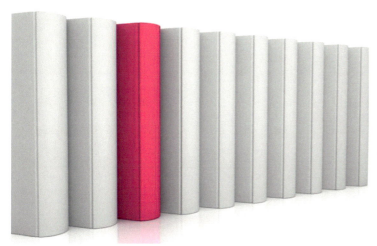

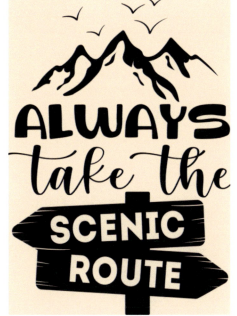

Always take the SCENIC ROUTE

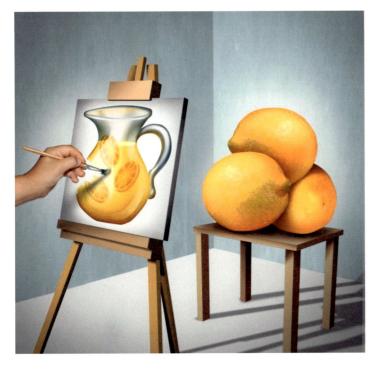

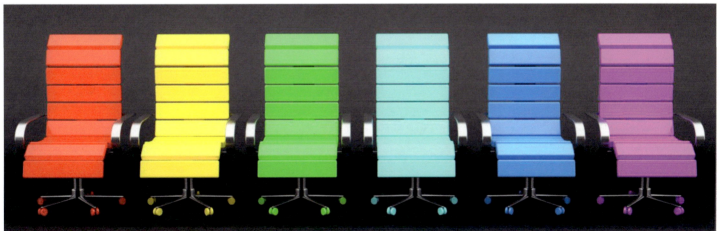

KEEP RAISING *the bar*

BOSS

PERSONAL GOALS

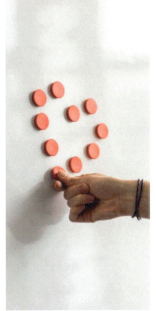

DECLARATION

IMPACT FACTOR

YOU ARE awesome

MAKE AN IMPACT

LiVE ON PURPOSE

breathe

Let it Go

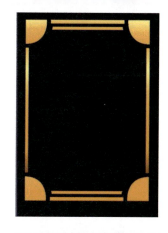

TEAMWORK

I WRITE MY OWN STORY

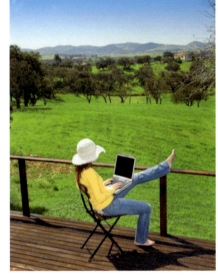

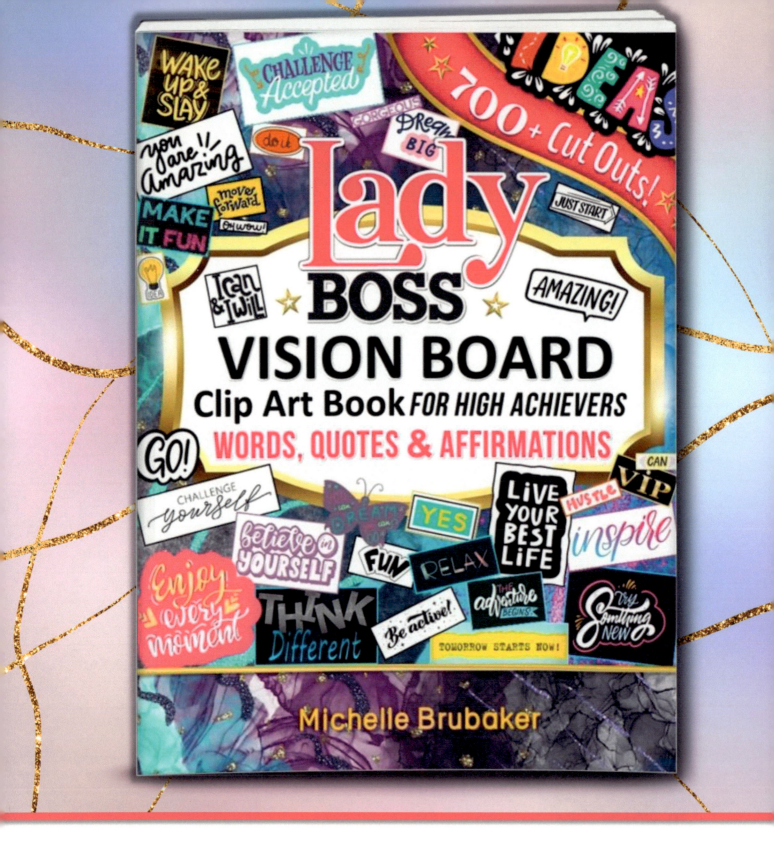

 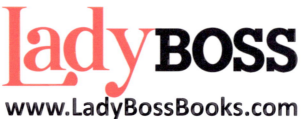

www.LadyBossBooks.com

Made in United States
Troutdale, OR
10/30/2024